THE

RESPONSIBILITY FOR PARTITION

CONSIDERED WITH AN EYE
TO IRELAND'S FUTURE

BY WILLIAM O'BRIEN

BooksUlster

First published by Maunsel & Roberts, Dublin, 1921. Second edition published by Books Ulster 2017.

Typographical arrangement © Books Ulster

ISBN: 978-1-910375-60-0

A FOREWORD

At the final stage of the Partition Bill ere it became law Mr. Bonar Law made the remarkable prediction: "This will not be the last Home Rule Bill." Hence the necessity for the present publication. It is not a lament for what is past, but a source of indispensable information for the future, if the Partition of Ireland is ever to be undone.

Most Rev. Dr. MacRory, Bishop of Down and Connor, the other day made a confession, which is a tragedy, viz., that "I am no longer in Ireland." The reason why is one which can now be recalled in temperate terms, but which cannot be ignored without eternising the Nationalist surrender by which Carson became the master of Ulster. In Bishop MacRory's own city of Belfast, a Convention of the Nationalists of the Six Counties was coerced into condoning the surrender under the threat of the resignation of the three Partitionist leaders and by other forms of coercion more disgraceful still. The cry was then that the move was a purely tactical one, and that Partition could never come to anything. Every warning to the contrary was for years derided, or was denounced as factionism. It may be that the fact that the diocese of Bishop MacRory and the archdiocese of Cardinal Logue are now actually "no longer in Ireland" by a law which (unlike the feeble Act of "the Home Rule Government") will be rigorously enforced may for the moment horrify the Nationalists of Ulster into a full realization of the politicians' arts by which they allowed themselves to be hypnotized. At this moment, however, the danger is present and even urgent. The men who wrung from the Belfast Convention the vote which is really responsible for the passing of the Partition Act have been condemned by their countrymen in a manner which ought to make any man of sensitive honour among them for ever hide his head. But their power for mischief is not even yet altogether exhausted. Under cover of the most ferocious military despotism unloosed upon Ireland for a century, they may calculate upon again some day finding an audience among the panic-stricken and the worthy people who, at every moment of stress, raise the feeble-witted cry of peace at any price. But experience ought at least to put a wise country on its guard against the possibility that the Hibernian politicians who entered into two several treaties for the Partition of Ireland, who had Mr. Lloyd George's bogus "Irish Convention" specially constructed for the purpose of making any other agreement except an agreement for Partition impossible, and who in the House of Commons abandoned all but the feeblest show of opposition to the Bill which repealed the Act of 1914 and gave legal recognition to Carson's Orange Free State, may be caught in some hour of national depression, in some insidious intrigue for actually working the Partition Act of which they are themselves the real authors. The *Times,* indeed, semi-officially announces that Sir Hamar Greenwood counts upon the elections to the Partitionist "Parliament" in Dublin being carried out for him by "the moderate elements of the community, including the old constitutional Nationalists under the leadership of Mr. John Dillon." It is even added, without any appearance of a joke, that *Sinn Féin* will obligingly clear out of their way, and "abstain." Be that as it may, it becomes of prime importance for the future to prove that the masses of the Irish people were kept plunged in the most melancholy ignorance of what was going on in Westminster in their name, and would have scouted the bare whisper of Partition as unspeakable treason to the nation if the statements and warnings embodied in the accompanying speeches had been allowed to come to their knowledge at the time.

The fatality by which a forty years' Home Rule movement ended in a measure not only defeating the demand of the Irish people for self-government, but establishing by express statutable enactment a new Orange and alien ascendancy over one-fourth of the country, will hereafter seem the most incomprehensible passage in Ireland's mournful history, unless the present amazing public ignorance on the subject can be dispelled. The Parliament of 1910 was elected for the fundamental object of "conferring full self-government upon Ireland." Nobody, least of all Sir E. Carson, proposed to split Ireland into two States. If Mr. Lloyd George had then publicly broached the "two-nation" theory which he has since forced into law, he could never have been a Minister of the Home Rule Government of 1910-16, and probably could not have found a seat in Parliament at all. The Home Rule majority in the House of Commons was supreme. It comprised (with only two exceptions) the full strength of the Liberal Party and of the Labour Party and eighty-one Irish Nationalists—a working majority which seldom or never fell below a hundred. A still greater and unprecedented advantage, the veto of the House of Lords, hitherto the death-stroke of every project of Irish freedom, was, by the explicit vote of the constituencies, reduced to impotence.

How came it that a Parliament with a mandate so direct and a power so overwhelming eventuated in the astounding result that "Ulster," whose war-cry was "We will not have Home Rule," is the only part of the country which obtain it, while the Irish race are not merely insulted by the refusal of their peaceful demand persisted in for more than a generation, but are ordered under terror of martial law to make themselves parties to the crime of splitting their ancient nation into two, and that by every device of racial and religious delimitation that could make the separation an irreparable one? The answer will, I think, be found within the brief compass of these pages.

For the destruction of Home Rule and the substitution of Partition the feebleness of most members of the Home Rule

Cabinet and the perfidy of others are no doubt primarily responsible. They could never have obtained their offices had they from the beginning avowed the designs which made the very first clause of their Home Rule Statute a living lie. But unhappily neither could they have retained their offices for a single week had not seventy-three of the eighty-one Nationalist representatives of Ireland allowed themselves to be made partners in the infamous scheme of Partition, even to the point of bargaining for their own instalment as the first Parliament of the separated Southern Ireland, without giving their constituents the smallest voice in electing them. The four speeches here reprinted, which were delivered in the presence of the Hibernian Parliamentary Party without any attempt on their part to refute them, are unanswerable proofs where the responsibility really lay.

Nor will it do to plead that their surrender was made under pressure of the Great War. The first bargain for the severance of the four counties of Antrim, Down, Armagh, and Derry was made months before there was any apprehension of a war. Still less will it avail to pretend that Partition was the work of a Coalition Government. Mr. Asquith and his Cabinet were in power when the Four Counties were surrendered and were in power still when twelve months later the surrender was extended to six counties. The moment the Home Rule Cabinet first whispered of Partition, the representatives of Ireland had the power of either insisting upon their recantation or ejecting them from office. They, on the contrary, voted steadily with the Partition Government and howled down as traitors the little group of Irish Nationalists who protested. Even when Mr. Asquith despatched his Home Rule Government and put a Coalition Ministry overwhelmingly Unionist in their place, the Hibernian Party raised not a voice in remonstrance but co-operated with the Coalitionists in forbidding any opportunity for even discussing the subject. A Parliamentary position such as no Irish leader had ever enjoyed before—not Grattan nor O'Connell nor Parnell—was surrendered without striking a blow. Carson, the gun-runner and potential rebel, was installed as the most formidable figure in the Ministry erected on the ruins of Home Rule; the members of the Hibernian Party became the most powerless items in the service of the Coalition. When the survivors of the Hibernian Party in the next Parliament made a farcical show of detestation of Partition, as it was finally passed by the Government of Mr. Lloyd George, the Prime Minister, Mr. Winston Churchill, and Mr. Bonar Law had no difficulty in silencing them by recalling that there was nothing in the new Partition Bill which they and their colleagues had not assented to as the condition for passing the old one.

Whenever the next legislative attempt is made to undo Partition, Ireland will undoubtedly be met with the taunt that not only her Parliamentary representatives, but the mass of her people, were consenting parties. It becomes a matter of sovereign importance to supply the explanation. It is, no doubt, true that the Hibernian Party could not have persevered in their ill-doing if Irish public opinion had not condoned their proceedings with a slavishness that might well seem to argue their unfitness for democratic self-government. It is only now that the reasons for their supineness can be revealed without injury to the Irish cause.

Public opinion was, if the brutal truth must be known, silenced on Irish platforms by boxwood batons, revolvers, and paving stones, and every attempt to convey the truth to the country by speeches in Parliament was frustrated by a ruthless boycott in the Press.

The two worst offenders in the Nationalist daily Press lived to receive a punishment that strangely fitted the crime. Their offices were raided with impartial irony by the Government of their idol, Mr. Lloyd George, and by the Irish Republican Army.

The directors and editor of one of them were fined £3,500, sentenced to jail for twelve months, and their offices set on fire; the other had its machinery blown up with gelignite—brutal methods both; intolerant and tyrannical methods to the last degree. But not a bit more foul or more opposed to the first principles of freedom than their own system, pursued for many years, of strangling the voice of every public man who strove to warn the country of the impending calamity which has since consigned Ireland to mourning and ruin.

Those who read the following pages by the light of subsequent events will scarcely dispute that if the warnings and arguments set forth in these speeches could have reached thoughtful men at the time in Ireland, Partition could never have been consummated. But of the four speeches in the House of Commons here republished it is certain that, outside the two or three Munster counties in which the *Cork Free Press* circulated, not a score of men in the country ever read them, or even heard of them except through some malignant misrepresentation. To the general reader they will be as new as if they never had been spoken. So completely had the species of Party Unity which proved to be the destruction of National Unity been turned into a perverted religion that under the rule of the Board of Erin Hibernians the mass of quiet citizens allowed themselves to be persuaded that the one condition of sure and instant triumph for Home Rule was a blind faith in the deceitful promises poured into their ears by the Party orators and the Party Press and an excommunication as a traitor of any man who should intimate the most modest dissent. There are few instances in history of popular credulity pushed to more pathetic extremes than the "joy-day" on which the dupes of the Board of Erin celebrated with bonfires the passage of the Act which was the legislative sanction of the Partition of the country and which has now been repealed without a cough in the way of real resistance by the men who passed it. These poor people knew not in the least what they did.

But a less humiliating defence of Irish self-respect is at hand. The laboriously organized bonfires of the Board of Erin were far less striking than the silence of death which overspread the country in general. People shrank from noisily protesting, but only half-informed though even thinking Irishmen were of what was happening, there were already hoarsely audible the rumblings of the earthquake which before many months were over was to lay the Hibernian Partition Party in ruins. The pretence that the Sinn Féin revolution was caused by the shooting of the rebel leaders of Easter Week or by the blunders of the War Office in the matter of Irish recruiting was like attributing the red outbreak of Vesuvius to a politicians' quarrel in some tavern at its base.

No immediate explosion of the country's indignation was possible. The Coalition Ministry took care that the Hibernian Party should not be compelled to face their constituents for two years after their mandate was exhausted. Year after year for seven years the Hibernian garrison of place-jobbers in the local governing bodies was kept similarly secure from the avenging arm of the electorate. The Partitionists seemed still so firm-seated, what with an inarticulate country and a Press manipulated with the ruthlessness of Thuggee, that it is not to be doubted that if they had triumphed at the bye-elections which preceded the General Election of 1918, they would have persisted in their Partitionist designs and finally accomplished them by means of Mr. Lloyd George's "Irish Convention." Providentially it was not to be. The conviction long burning in the country's breast that the fairest opportunity Ireland was ever blest with had been destroyed by men who had substituted Partition and a nationality narrowed by a pseudo-Catholic sacramental test for the historic ideals of our nation asserted itself with an ever-growing power at the North Roscommon, East Clare, South Longford, and Kilkenny bye-elections, and when the avalanche of the General Election at last arrived there were left barely two of the seventy-three Hibernian Partitionists as the only survivors elected by free Irish votes.

That is the answer to the argument that the Irish nation through their representatives were consenting parties to the Partition surrender now inscribed upon the Statute Book. The moment the Irish nation could make its voice heard the Partitionists were dismissed all but to a man from Ireland's service, and dismissed for ever. The discredit which they brought upon themselves by long years of malfeasance was gradually extended to Parliamentary methods in general. A new programme and new men have definitely taken command of the Irish cause. To the new leaders who rescued the country from a pit of corruption and self-seeking, our race will, I make no doubt, give a prolonged and generous measure of the allegiance they all-too-patiently extended to their predecessors who wrought the ignominious destruction of Parnell's great movement. Whatever may be the new men's difficulties in budging an inch towards peace under the appalling conditions now existing, I do not apprehend that their statesmanship will, in the long run, be found to be inferior in wisdom to their firmness, purity of purpose, and unbounded sacrificial heroism. English politicians would do well to realize that all attempts to divide the country by touting for peace plenipotentiaries other than those of the Parliament of Ireland, elected in 1918, are foredoomed to failure. Whenever the final reckoning between the two countries comes to be cast up, the one prediction that may be safely hazarded is that the Partition Act now inscribed upon the Statute-book will by an equally general consent and contempt go the way of the "Act on the Statute-book" by which the Hibernian Partitionists for years fooled Irish credulity to the top of its bent. That result may not impossibly be hastened by the demonstration that the speeches now re-printed, which were spoken in the name of only eight

Irish Nationalists in a House of Commons raucous with the jeers and derision of Ireland's own so-called representatives, spoke really the deepest mind and purpose of our race, and are now the commonplaces of Ireland's present thoughts and future hopes.

WILLIAM O'BRIEN.

MALLOW, JAN. 1ST, 1921.

I

THE WARNING

[Speech delivered on April 1st, 1914, in debate on Second Reading of Bill for the Better Government of Ireland.]

MR. WILLIAM O'BRIEN—The Foreign Minister (Sir Edward Grey) in his grave speech of last evening made two things plain which strangely escaped the attention of the hon. member for East Mayo (Mr. Dillon), who has just spoken, but which will not escape attention in Ireland. The first is that in this year, which has been christened the Home Rule year, there will be no Home Rule for Ireland, nor even for three-quarters of Ireland.

The next thing the Foreign Minister made clear is that there never will be an Irish Parliament at all, nor even a three-quarters Irish Parliament, unless and until England gives her leave at the General Election, which the people of Ireland were assured a thousand times over would never come off again under the present conditions.

The only comfort the Foreign Minister could give to the Redmondite Party, whom the learned Solicitor-General has just described as "his followers," is that the Government will go through the farce of nominally placing on the Statute Book this dummy Bill, which you have offered to transform in its most vital particular, and which you confess you have not the least intention of putting into force without that appeal to England, which it was the strongest recommendation of the Parliament Act that it would enable us to avoid. Sir, if under such circumstances, the Government go through the ghastly farce of nominally passing this Bill,

It will be an imposture at the expense of the Irish people in order to save the face of the Government's Hibernian "followers."

I cannot congratulate either the Government or Ireland or England upon any of those recent developments.

You may have postponed the trouble in Ulster, but you have demoralized your Army; you have swelled the heads of the Covenanters, and you have ruined your Irish Settlement without pleasing anybody.

That at all events is my profound conviction. I don't know which to admire the least—the levity with which the Government adopted this plan of dismemberment, without even thinking it out, or the alacrity with which they more than half dropped it at Bradford, or the third change of front, when the Prime Minister announced that they still stood by the "principle":—

What he calls a principle being what we call the absolute negation of the first principle of Irish Nationality, the only principle which makes this Bill worth fighting for.

Or the final change of front, when you marched your army up the hill in Ulster, and then marched them down again—that is, so far as you can get them to march at all. (Laughter.) Sir, all those military alarms and excursions in Ulster and at the Curragh and in Downing Street, may be, and undoubtedly are, matters of the most painful interest to the people of Great Britain. I do deeply sympathise with them in their anxieties on the subject.

But for Irish Nationalists all other questions are now overshadowed by the fact that for the first time even in our unhappy History, a Majority of Ireland's own representatives have consented to the partition of our Country.

The only consolation administered to us in Ireland was the whisper that went around that the offer of exclusion was deliberately framed in order to be rejected. And that the Unionists would oblige us by promptly flinging it back in the Government's teeth. Sir, this is not what has happened. The Unionists have gone very far indeed towards the acceptance of that offer. And the Foreign Minister last night announced that the Government are still pinned to the principle as well as to certain unspecified details as to which we can know nothing until we hear the next surrender by the Party who sit behind me.

In fact, the danger at the present moment, is that both English Parties will agree only too well, in a bargain that will divide the oyster between them, and present the Irish people with the empty oyster shells. Because, let there be no mistake about it, this debate is no longer a question of reconciling Ireland by a satisfactory measure of Home Rule, it is purely and simply a question of saving England from Civil War at the expense of Ireland.

Apparently the Government and their Hibernian "followers" were at first a little daunted at the consternation their proposal aroused in Ireland, but they seem now to have made up their minds that Ireland does not matter—that Ireland will stand anything. Well, sir, I quite admit that Mr. Dillon had perhaps some ground for his boast as to the silence of the grave that hangs over the greater part of Ireland. Ireland has never come nearer to deserving Byron's description of

"A bastinadoed elephant kneeling to receive its paltry rider."

Public opinion in Ireland at this moment is repressed under the heel of a powerful Secret Society—(Redmondite interruptions)—**and of a Corrupt Place-Hunting Press as rigorously as under any English Coercion Act I have known, and I have known a good many. But, sir, there is a point at which the discontent that has been driven under the surface will burst loose, and may give the member for East Mayo some startling surprises.**

The Bishop of Kildare, who is a supporter of the member for Waterford, tells us that he himself heard this offer with the feelings of a man who is informed that his leg would have to be amputated above the knee. His lordship, no doubt, tells us that the poor people will submit in "sullen acquiescence"—a cheerful frame of mind for a people who are assured that they are on the eve of the recovery of their National freedom.

But let not the member for East Mayo be too sure that this policy of amputation above the knee may not before many months are over rouse the Irish race to a state of mind considerably more lively than "sullen acquiescence."

The Foreign Minister told us last night that he will not go beyond the six years limit for the exclusion of Ulster, but he held the door open for some arrangement by which the length of the time-limit would depend upon the passing of some general scheme of Federalism.

Sir, I shall not be an opponent of any well-considered scheme of Federalism.

I am not at all sure that it will not be found ultimately to be the only practical solution. (Ministerial cheers.) But it must be understood clearly that we will have no Federal Scheme which is based upon the separation of Ulster from the rest of Ireland as a *fait accompli.*

But, sir, I regard this distinction between a six-year limit and perpetual exclusion as a disgusting fraud and sham.

Mr. Winston Churchill—As what?

Mr. O'Brien—As a disgusting fraud and sham. It imposes on nobody in Ireland—this notion of resurrecting the amputated limb after six years.

If Ireland is once divided with the consent of her own representatives, she will remain divided.

Indeed, the member for Waterford regards exclusion as so

comparatively insignificant a matter that at the Patrick's Day banquet he actually spoke of it as on the same level with the reservation of the Royal Irish Constabulary.

> **In the very act of speaking to the toast of Ireland a Nation, he actually talked as if dispensing with the control of a British military force which never belonged to us, as if it stood on the same footing as the amputation from the body of Ireland of four or five or six Counties, every mile of which is watered with the blood of her most heroic defenders of the two races and of the two creeds.**

He actually talked as if in six years it would be as simple a matter to whistle back a victorious Orange Free State into his Dublin Parliament as it would be to induce the Royal Irish Constabulary to exchange one paymaster for another. The member for East Mayo (Mr. Dillon) went still further. He discovered the materials for a Te Deum in this exclusion of Ulster.

> **Mr. Dillon, who figured so ardently as a Conciliationist to-day, has been for the past ten years the deadliest enemy of Conciliation in Ireland. And it is woeful to think that he only turns Conciliationist now upon the basis of a dismemberment which would blot out the very name of Ireland as a Nation.**

Speaking at Newcastle a few days ago he said: "I have no hesitation in saying that so far as I am concerned this offer is an honest offer, and I pray to God they might accept it." Well, sir, although he was only speaking in England, I might almost have believed him that the exclusion of Ulster has now become the object of his pious prayers to the Almighty, only that unfortunately he speaks with two voices. He repeated here to-night for the comfort of the Unionists his declaration—"As regards the question of the time-limit, the Irish Party recognized that they were running great risks because in the not unlikely contingency of the Tory Party returning to power in the next six years it would be possible for them by a one-clause Bill to make the exclusion perpetual."

But with an adroitness and a discretion all his own, he told an Irish audience in the North of England a few days previously—"If at a future election the Tory Party were to come back into power and were to decree that the exclusion of Ulster would be perpetual, what would be the result? The Irish Government and the Irish members would immediately take up the gage of battle and we would fight again with an united Ireland."

That is a pretty picture of the Millennium. (Laughter.) In other words he tells the Tories in one breath that nothing will be easier than perpetual exclusion, and in the next that his Dublin Parliament and himself will resist it to the death.

Sir, the hon. member must forgive me if I attach more importance to the danger of the one-clause Bill than to his valiant threats of resistance to exclusion. The only successful resistance he offered in his life was to the National policy to which the entire Irish Party and the entire Irish Nation were solemnly pledged, and which only for him would long ago have brought this question to a happy solution without a shot being fired or an angry word said in Ulster.

Sir, the member for Waterford's prayers go rather in the direction of the Unionists relieving him by rejecting this offer. Because in that event I remember with what a majestic wave of the hand he announced that nothing would be easier than to go on with the Bill as it stands and to put down force with force.

In that I think he was as wise and as far-seeing as when he told the country a short time ago that there was no longer an Ulster Difficulty.

The matter is not quite so simple as that, as the Government have since found out with heavy hearts. I am glad to see the First Lord of the Admiralty (Mr. Winston Churchill) in his place. It was his unlucky visit to Belfast which was the beginning of all this Ulster trouble. (All-for-Ireland and Opposition cheers and Radical interruptions.) Gentlemen opposite know little of Belfast, or they would not doubt it. The First Lord has since boxed the entire compass on this subject. From his first raid on the Ulster Hall to his recantation at Dundee and then to his speech in Bradford, when he recanted his Recantation and invoked the God of Battle, and promised "to put those grave matters to the proof."

Sir, he has since "put those grave matters to the proof," and the result is those "honest misunderstandings" in Ulster and at the Curragh and in Downing Street, with which we are only too painfully familiar.

In his speech at Bradford the First Lord used these words—"Bloodshed, gentlemen, no doubt, is lamentable, but there are worse things than bloodshed even on an extreme scale."

Sir, I cannot think that the First Lord can have guessed what a shudder he sent to the hearts of those of us who have given our lives to creating a genuinely United Ireland.

It is not the enemies of this Bill in Ulster whom he has frightened. "Bloodshed on an extreme scale" may seem a comparatively small matter to a War Lord or a Sea Lord, but if once Irish blood were shed in this way, by Englishmen or by Irishmen, it would poison the entire life of Ireland for a generation to come like another Battle of the Boyne.

I condemn and abhor with all my heart those military preparations of the Covenanters, for even the possibility of the slaughter of Irishmen by Irishmen.

(Ministerial cheers). They are, to my mind, outrageously illegal, and are ridiculously disproportioned to any disastrous consequences that could follow to Ulster from this somewhat paltry Dublin Parliament. But if anybody is to be arraigned, I am afraid the so-called Government of Ireland and their Hibernian advisers will have to be joined in the indictment. The Foreign Minister (Sir E. Grey) last night complained of the difficulties put in the way of all the concessions offered by the Government. The Foreign Minister himself is no doubt honourably distinguished by the efforts he has made for a settlement by consent, but with that one exception, what are the concessions the Government have ever offered until those last few weeks, when they have made an offer of dismemberment, which is hateful to every man, woman, and child in Ireland. (All-for-Ireland and Opposition cheers). They had two years to think over the concessions which they have offered at last, but in the utterly wrong direction.

They conceded nothing; they only jibed and jested.

Two years ago there was not a mouse stirring in Ulster, and the Unionist Party were not yet committed. If two years ago, even six months ago, they had taken Lord Loreburn's advice and called into Council the best men of all parties—of whom the right hon. member who proposed this amendment (Mr. Walter Long) and the Foreign Minister himself are undoubtedly among the highest types—and if they had even failed to reach an agreement and had boldly gone to the country, upon their concessions, as they now will have to do, with less grace and with less merit, nothing would have been easier than to have suppressed this military association within a month and to punish like ordinary citizens any high and mighty personages who might persist in it. (Ministerial cheers.)

Your opportunity is lost. You have both done too much and done too little.

(Opposition cheers.) It is too late to do that now, without that "bloodshed on an extreme scale," which the First Lord contemplated with Napoleonic serenity, but which no matter how prompt or how bloody was the victory of your troops, would turn into a ghastly sarcasm the title of this Bill for the Better Government of Ireland. The Government are now trying to make up for their astounding want of foresight in dealing with one-fourth of the Irish population, by rushing into the opposite extreme, and offering a concession which throws the remaining three-fourths of the population into a state of "sullen indignation," which scandalises all Irishmen alike,

> **And which is as much execrated in Belfast as it is in Cork. That is what your new system of the Government of Ireland by a Secret Conspiracy has brought you to. You have allowed one Secret Conspiracy to lead you by the nose, and you have allowed the other Secret Conspiracy to intimidate you.**

Mr. Speaker, I have never criticised without endeavouring to offer some alternative. Look where I will, I can see only one way of escape, for the Government, or for the Unionists, or for Ireland. (Radical interruptions.) Gentlemen opposite ought really to remember that it is not their own country, but ours they are cutting in pieces. (All-for-Ireland cheers.)

I wonder what would be their own feelings if Germany proposed to give them the whole of England, but to reserve the County of Middlesex as a German Ulster on the ground that the Anglo-Saxons had long ago come over from Germany. The thing is not at all impossible.

> **Sir, what I want to say is that in my view the only way out of the difficulty is for the Government to retrace their steps, to abandon honestly this hateful plan for the break-up of Ireland, and to invite some small body of dispassionate, representative men to devise some better solution.**

They have hit upon the one concession which scandalizes all Irishmen. Is there no other, no better, form of conciliation?

> **The Prime Minister, in unfolding this hopelessly bad plan to the House, confessed he was himself convinced that there was another and a better solution, and if I un-**

**derstood the Foreign Minister rightly, last night—he
can correct me if I am wrong—he is also of the same
opinion.**

(Sir Edward Grey nodded his head). The Prime Minister, after
speaking of those minor local concessions which are known as
Home Rule within Home Rule, went on to say—"Then as regards legislation, my proposal was this—and I am still rather
wedded to it, though I am afraid I met with very little support
in any quarter—that Ulster should return, like all the rest of Ireland, representatives to both the Upper and the Lower Houses
of the Irish Legislature, but that when any law was passed by
those two Houses to which in respect of its application to Ulster
the majority of the representatives of Ulster were opposed, it
should not come into force *quoad* Ulster, if they protested, until
it received the sanction of the Imperial Parliament. That, I think,
was going a very long way—a very much longer way than many
people expected or desired.

**I gather it receives very little support in any part of this
House,**

but it had this advantage, that, in the first place, it completely
met the question of possible administrative oppression; in the
next place, it started Ireland with a fully representative Irish Parliament; and in the third place it preserved the veto of the Imperial Parliament in regard to legislation which might injuriously
affect the Ulster minority—preserved it, not only as it is in the
Bill when it can only be exercised on the initiative of the Imperial Parliament itself, but preserved, or rather extended it, in such
a form that it could at any time be brought into operation upon
the initiative of a majority of Ulster Members. I am not going to
press that suggestion upon the House. I part from it myself with
regret and with reluctance, but it has one drawback, and a very
serious drawback. It does not commend itself to any of the parties concerned. That was the first road which we pursued—or, at

any rate, which I pursued—in the direction of peace."

Sir, it is a misfortune that the Prime Minister should be absent from the House at this present critical stage of this great controversy. (General cheers.) If he were here I should like to ask him what was the influence which compelled him to part reluctantly with the solution, which he believed to be the best one. When the Prime Minister says— "I gather it receives little support in any part of this House," I want to know from him or from the Foreign Minister what steps were taken to test the feeling of this House beyond secret conversations with half-a-dozen Party managers, and this is not a question for Party wire-pullers, but for millions of men. Above all, what steps were taken to test the feeling of the Protestant minority in Ireland themselves? Sir, I am afraid I will be able to satisfy the House that

The real opposition came from the Hibernian Party, and that it was because the substance of this concession came originally from my colleagues and myself that they over-rode the Prime Minister's own feeling as to the best road to peace, and forced him to the alternative of disruption, which is incomparably more humiliating for Ireland and is absolutely destructive of this Bill as a measure of settlement between these two countries.

When I was forced to take the opinion of the people of the City of Cork lately, I did so in a public letter headed, "What the Cork Election will mean," and that letter began: "I desire to set forth in precise terms the programme of Conciliation on which I intend to stand or fall in the election which Mr. Redmond's official representatives have forced upon the City of Cork." I need not trouble the House with certain other concessions I suggested, such as doubling the representation of the Irish minority in the Irish Parliament, and disposing of public offices according to merit, and not according to the signs and passwords of a secret society. I will read only the first paragraph, because I think you will find it almost identical with the proposal which has since commended itself to the Prime Minister and to the Foreign Minister as the happiest solution:—

"(The Ulster terror of parting with the active authority of the Imperial Parliament.) We propose, for an experimental term of five years, to give the Ulster Party which would remain in the Imperial Parliament (say ten, with the possible addition of two members, one for Trinity College and one for Rathmines, to represent the Southern minority) a direct suspensory veto upon any Bill of the Irish Parliament unless and until it shall either be approved or rejected by a resolution of the Imperial Parliament to be passed within a month after the exercise of the veto. Further, to give the Ulster Party the right upon a signed requisition to the Speaker of discussing on a motion for the adjournment of the House of Commons, any administrative Act of the Irish Executive dealing with Education, Justice or Police. For the experimental period, these powers would give the Protestant minority the direct and active protection of the Imperial Parliament in a much more effectual way than they possess it at present. Such a suspensory veto may seem an unheard of concession to a minority, and so it is. It would, in my judgment, be gladly submitted to by the best thinking men of our race, in the belief that it would serve as a wholesome restraint upon an infant Parliament in its first inexperienced years, and in the firm conviction that nothing will be attempted which would either tempt the Ulster Party to exercise the veto or the Imperial Parliament to enforce it."

The House will have perceived that that is substantially the proposal of the Prime Minister except that the Prime Minister confines himself to Ulster, while we propose to extend the protection to the minority in other parts of Ireland, whose anxieties I confess appeal more closely to my sympathies. Also the Prime Minister left the veto one of indeterminate length, while we proposed that the whole thing should be settled one way or another, within one month and by a simple resolution of the Imperial Parliament.

Sir, how was that proposal treated by the Hibernian Liberal Party, not, of course, here in England, where they are more cautious, but by their paid organisers and subsidised newspapers in Ireland?

In the first place, they suppressed my letter bodily. That they had a perfect right to do if they did not misrepresent it. But while they suppressed every other line of that letter, they picked out one sentence from the paragraph which I have just read to you, in order, as I shall show you, most grossly to garble my proposal. They dreaded to let their supporters know what I really proposed.

They dreaded to face the people in the secrecy of the Ballot, when upon their insolent challenge I invited them to do so upon those very Concessions.

They hypocritically pretended it would be a National scandal to take the verdict of the people in the only constitutional way in two great Nationalist constituencies, but they think it no National scandal at all in a moment like this to proclaim a war of extermination, not merely against us members of Parliament, but against every County Councillor and District Councillor in the South who have adhered to the policy of Conciliation, which the member for East Mayo (Mr. Dillon) preached so unctuously here to-night.

These many hundreds of representative men over half a Province are to be exterminated, not because they neglected their duties as County Councillors and District Councillors, but because they have held by the Concessions in which the Prime Minister and the Foreign Minister discern the best hope of a permanent settlement between these two countries.

Accordingly they have undertaken with all their funds and with

all the foul weapons of their Secret Society, to, in their own fa-
vourite phrase, "wipe off the face of the earth" those thousands
of better Nationalists than themselves, I suppose by way of fore-
taste of those miracles of loving kindness by which they undertake to win over the Covenanters of the North in six years. The
Freeman's Journal way of putting it is that it is to be a holy war
to "wipe out the blot of factionism." (Redmondite cheers and
interruptions.) Yes, there goes the chorus. I only wonder they
have not the courage to raise here their usual war-cry of "Up the
Mollies."

**But, Sir, what is the Factionism these men are making war
upon? Factionism means every Irish Nationalist who
dares to raise his voice against the ring of secret society bosses.** (Redmondite and Radical interruptions)—**and
Dublin Castle Placehunters who are butchering the
cause of Ireland.** (All-for-Ireland cheers and Redmondite
interruptions.) **And what is this "Freeman's Journal"? It
is the Patriot Journal, which has quartered no less than
sixteen members of its staff in Dublin Castle jobs from
the Lord Chancellor down since the present Government came into office.**

(All-for-Ireland and Opposition cheers.) And, Sir, what is the
pretext for this campaign of vengeance? They picked out one
sentence from the paragraph I have read to you—wrenched it
from its context— and on the strength of it, they have appealed
to the basest and most bigoted passions on the cry that I propose to hand over Ireland to the veto of ten Orangemen.

**The veto of ten Orangemen! I ask any fair man who has
heard this paragraph, was there ever a more disgraceful
misrepresentation?**

In the first place, so far as I know, there are not more than three
members of the Ulster Party who are members of the Orange
Order. What I do know is that in the course of these debates I

have heard at least four of them confess that upon our lines the consent of Ulster might and would be won, and a pretty way has been taken of encouraging them. Even Sir Edward Carson, who is listening to me, said very much the same in Belfast a day or two ago.

But what I proposed was to give a suspensory veto for one month only not to ten Orangemen, but to the elected representatives of more than a million of the Irish people, and I proposed it with limitations which would make it all but certain that the veto would never be exercised because of the very completeness of the protection it would afford, and because the immediate action of this House would punish any unreasonable exercise of the veto. (General cheers.)

The hon. member for Scotland Division (Mr. T. P. O'Connor), with his customary obliging candour to opponents, confessed in a speech the other day that there are more vetoes in this Bill than there are padlocks in a jail. That is perfectly true. It is a pretty commentary upon this Bill as a great measure of National freedom. But the hon. member and his friends never in the least objected to the Veto of the Lord Lieutenant, to the Veto of the Imperial Parliament, to the Veto of the Privy Council, or to the Veto of the Joint Exchequer Board.

All these Vetoes will be exercised by aliens, but the moment it is a question of allaying the apprehensions of one-fourth of our own countrymen, the co-religionists of Grattan and Parnell and Mitchel and Butt, whom the Member for East Mayo plastered with his praises here to-night, the Hibernian Liberals are horrified at a Veto for a single month, and denounce the representatives of one million of the Irish people as ten Orangemen,

although I heard the member for Waterford in the course of these debates repeat an old saying of O'Connell, which, I confess, goes further than I would be prepared to go, that he would rather have Ireland governed by the worst Orangeman than by the best Englishman. Sir, that is the secret why the solution, which the Prime Minister and the Foreign Minister believe in, has been forbidden and destroyed, as Lord Loreburn's proposal for a Conference was destroyed before that.

The Secret is that the Concession had the misfortune to come from us.

And these are the gentlemen who have without a scruple consented to rend asunder the Ireland that we have known and laboured for—to divide her by Statute into two countries, two races, and two religions, and all upon the cheerful calculation that in six years they will capture the hearts of the Covenanters of Ulster by the gentle arts they are practising for the extermination of every County Councillor and District Councillor in the South who has dared to make the word Conciliation anything better than a hypocritical sham and fraud. (All-for-Ireland and Opposition cheers.) Mr. Speaker, we shall probably have still two months before the final word is spoken on this controversy at the polls. The Foreign Minister (Sir E. Grey) last night said: "That time might still be used in investigating whether there is not yet a chance that some measure of agreement may be reached." God forbid that we should stand in the way of such a spirit. I would respectfully entreat the Prime Minister (Mr. Asquith) and the Foreign Minister to do justice to their high repute for statesmanship, which in their case, at all events, has come untarnished through the squalid transactions of the last few weeks and to return to the proposals which they "abandoned with reluctance and regret."

Let them not be afraid of the people and especially of the Irish people. When it came to be a question of facing the people's verdict in the ballot in two great Nationalist constituencies, the other day, we know what became of

the men who accused me of handing Ireland over to the veto of ten Orangemen. Note—The elections for Cork City and the North Division of Cork County, where All-for-Ireland candidates were returned unopposed.

The same thing, I am firmly convinced, would happen with the great mass of the Irish people, Catholics and Protestants, if they were tested in the only reliable way. Let us, at all events, have the merits of these two conflicting programmes—the programme of contracting out and the programme of contracting in—the programme of uniting Ireland and the programme of deliberately dividing Ireland —threshed out as they have never yet been by the best men of all parties, and even if no agreement can be come to, let the Government then straightforwardly appeal to the country for the power which they certainly have not now, but before which any armed resistance in Ulster or elsewhere must instantly collapse. (Ministerial cheers.)

As to the lines you are at present travelling upon, they will bring you to nothing except division and disaster between the two countries. So far from appeasing the national sentiment, which it was the object of this Bill to appease, you have inflicted upon the dearest aspiration of the Irish people a wound for which they will not forgive you for many a year to come.

Even if we should be a small minority of Irishmen in this House in resisting this proposal, as we shall resist it with every weapon of Parliamentary procedure—even if Ireland is for the moment so dragooned as to submit "in sullen acquiescence," a time will come when that sullen acquiescence will be shaken off, and you will be made to rue the day when you ever touched this fatal and criminal conspiracy against the unification of Ireland as a Nation.

II

A FINAL PROTEST
BEFORE HISTORY

[Speech delivered on May 25th, 1914, on the final stage of the Home Rule Bill in the House of Commons, when the Bill was accompanied by Mr. Asquith's solemn guarantee that it would never be enforced without an Amending Bill, enacting the Separation of the Six Counties. This speech was the only word of protest uttered by a representative of Ireland. When the All-for-Irelanders, as a final protest before History, followed it up by abstaining from voting for a Bill which had become a Partition Bill, they were assailed with yells of "Factionists!" and "Traitors!" by the Hibernian Party, whose own votes had just pledged Ireland's fatal consent to the Partition infamy.]

Mr. William O'Brien—Mr. Speaker, I am sorry to be obliged for a very few minutes to stand between the House and an immediate division, but, notwithstanding the breakdown of this debate, and in fact all the more on that account, it is not possible for those whom we represent in this House to avoid some expression of our views as to the wholly altered conditions under which this Bill is now presented for a third reading. The Prime Minister (Mr. Asquith) has done all that eloquence and ingenuity could do to put the best face on the transaction, but I must own that this strategy of secrecy in this House as to the grave nature of the Amending Bill under the pretext of sparing the feelings of the

House of Lords, is, in my opinion, an indefensible course. It is not straight dealing either with Ireland or with England. But I am convinced that if the Prime Minister has been driven to these methods of shuffling and mystification in reference to so vital a matter, it is because the course his own better judgment would have suggested has been made impossible for him by the Party who sit behind me (the Redmondites). This strategy of resurrecting the House of Lords as a sort of electioneering bogey in order to conceal the truth from Ireland somehow conveyed to me the impression of the last desperate throw of ruined gamblers.

The game was lost for Ireland the day when the honourable member for Waterford and his friends consented to the Partition of Ireland.

(All-for-Ireland cheers and Radical interruptions). That fact will never be forgotten for them, and will not easily be forgiven to them in spite of the cheers with which their treason is received on the Radical benches opposite. (All-for-Ireland cheers.) All that has happened since is only a consequence of their policy of

Bitterly opposing any genuine concession to Ulster at the right time, and now consenting to the concession of all others which will not only fail to conciliate Ulster, but will rouse millions of the Irish race in revolt against your Bill, and indeed against all British Party politicians impartially.

We all know the object of this policy of adjournment of any particulars to the House of Lords is to put off for a few weeks more the inevitable day of final disillusion for the unfortunate Irish people, and to enable the member for Waterford in the meantime to brag that some tremendous victory has been gained by the ghastly farce of this third reading to-night. It was only the other night the member for Waterford burst into an eloquent ecstasy which, if it meant anything at all, meant that the technical passage of this Bill will be the realization of all those glorious hopes of Ireland's freedom for which he told us he and his fathers have made such immeasurable sacrifices. (Laughter.) I should like to be in a position to cross-examine the learned member as to where on earth the victory for Ireland's freedom is to come in.

The Government are determined to pass this Bill, but they are equally determined not to put it in force in its most vital particular (All-for Ireland cheers),
while we got as far as the final passage through this House of a Home Rule Bill twenty-one years ago, and we got thus far in spite of the bitter hostility of the learned member for Waterford at that time towards Mr. Gladstone's far more generous Home Rule Bill of 1893.

The Prime Minister has confessed only a few minutes ago that this Bill is only a first instalment, and that the second instalment is to nullify the first.
We have heard of a certain preamble that never came off—(Opposition laughter)—but here we have a Bill the postscript to which is more important than the Bill itself, because it reduces the Bill to nothingness.

Any Bill that proposes to cut off Ulster permanently or temporarily from the body of Ireland is to me worse than nothingness, and I think you will find millions of Irish Nationalists will be of the same opinion. (All-for-Ireland cheers.)
The member for Waterford spoke as if the technical passage of this Bill will be a joy-day for Ireland as a nation. Sir, it will be, on the contrary, one of the grossest frauds that ever was perpetrated upon a too confiding Irish people.

It will be little short of a cruel practical joke at the expense of their intelligence as well as of their freedom. (All-for-Ireland cheers.)
They will have the cup of liberty presented to their lips, but only on condition that their lips must not touch it. They will be presented with a Bill which will declare in its first clause that all Ireland will henceforth be ruled by an Irish Parliament, but the very men who pass it declare that it will be nothing of the kind, and that

This lying statement will only be enacted in order to be repealed.

This Act, if ever it be an Act, will be born with a rope round its neck. It is not even intended to be enforced.

It is to be repudiated by its own authors in the particular of all others which wounds Irish Nationalism to the heart, and which will blot out the very name of Ireland as a nation. (All-for-Ireland cheers.)

Sir, the difference between us and the Party who sit behind us is that

We are ready for almost any conceivable concession to Ulster that will have the effect of uniting Ireland, but we will struggle to our last breath against a proposal which will divide her, and divide her eternally, if Ireland's own representatives are once consenting parties. (All-for-Ireland cheers.)

The learned member for Waterford has, no doubt, some right to boast that the Irish people have been trustful, if I should not say credulous, to the verge of tragedy. They have been so because the masses of the Irish people have been kept in a still more tragic ignorance of the A B C of the situation by a corrupted Press. (Radical and Redmondite interruptions.)

Well, I call a corrupted newspaper a newspaper that is bought by sixteen Government jobs for its staff.

(All-for-Ireland cheers.) But the learned member for Waterford may possibly find that

There are limits even to the gullibility of the poor people, who solemnly believed him when he assured them that there is no longer an Ulster difficulty.

(All-for-Ireland and Opposition cheers and laughter)—and that the last obstacle to Home Rule was gone when the Parliament Act was passed. (Opposition cheers and laughter.) His promises are already beginning to be at as hopeless a discount in Ireland as his veiled threats the other night to the Ministry whom he has led into the boghole in which we all find ourselves floundering at the present moment.

If you pass this Bill without the Amending, or rather the Repealing, Bill, it will be a farce too bitter for words, because you know you cannot enforce it until you have first got forty or fifty thousand rifles out of the hands of the Ulster Volunteers,

and nobody any longer dreams—not even the First Lord of the Admiralty (Mr. Winston Churchill)— that that is now practicable politics. Even were it otherwise, your success in beating down Ulster would be a scarcely less disastrous blow to the future of a united Ireland—(general cheers)—than if you failed again and repeated your performance of March last when the First Lord "put these grave matters to the test" and then took to his heels.

On the other hand if you do not enforce this Bill until the Repealing Bill is passed at practically the same time,

well, then, let us drop the canting pretext that you are satisfying Ireland's struggles for freedom and for national unity by splitting the country up into two rival and separate States, which will have no less than three separate minorities on their hands in a condition of discontent, and anger, and revolt, in place of the one minority we are dealing with at present. Of course we all know you have the voting power to pass this Bill as a sort of mechanical toy to amuse a people whom you very stupidly suppose to be a nation of children. But you know that this Bill does not mean business. (All-for-Ireland and Opposition cheers.) And so long as it is clogged as the Prime Minister to-night admits that it is clogged, by a Ministerial pledge of a repealing Bill for the mutilation of Ireland, we regard this Bill as no longer a Home Rule Bill, but as a Bill for the murder of Home Rule as we have understood it all our lives, and we can have no hand, act or part in the operation. (Loud All-for-Ireland cheers.)

III

THE "TEMPORARY AND PROVISIONAL" SHAM BLOWN SKY HIGH

[Speech delivered on 25th July, 1916, on Mr. Redmond's motion for the Adjournment of the House to call attention to the breakdown of the new "Headings of Agreement" for the Surrender of the Six Counties.]

Mr. William O'Brien—I have no right to interfere in the lovers' quarrel between the Member for Waterford and his old Liberal Allies or Masters. No doubt the Secretary for War (Mr. Lloyd George) has had the best of the honourable member and his Party in this transaction, as well as in all the rest of their sinister relations with him for the last six years. But I have a strong suspicion that

If the Minister for War has run away from the phraseology of these Headings of Agreement the member for Waterford and his friends have under pressure from Ireland run away from the substance of their bargain for the Partition of Ireland.

The member for Waterford's performance to-night was painfully reminiscent of the famous change of front in reference to the Irish Council Bill. There was the same readiness to change one set of views for the contrary within the shortest notice as soon as it was quite clear how the cat was jumping. Every allowance must be made for the member for Waterford. He never understood much about Ireland or about Irish Nationalist feeling.

It has taken almost a Second Irish Rising to convince him how dangerously the tide of indignation is rising in Ireland.

But apparently the only resource that is left him now is to pick a quarrel with the Government upon any pretext in order to extricate his friends and himself from their mess by pitiful hair-splitting about the phraseology of the original agreement with the Minister for War (Mr. Lloyd George), a document of which he took care not to give us the full and honest text. But, Sir, it is too late for the hon. member either to retreat or to advance in this matter.

The one point about this Agreement which all the water in the sea will never wash out is that he and his Party agreed to the Separation from Ireland of six of her richest and most historic counties, and of one-third of the entire Irish population, under conditions which nobody except a quibbler or a fool could represent as either temporary or provisional. That is the only point in all this disputation as to the wording of the Agreement in which the Irish people will take a farthing's worth of interest and that is the point which they will never forget nor forgive.

I really thought we had heard the last of this twaddle about the amputation of Ulster from the body of Ireland being a strictly temporary and provisional operation. That kind of thing will never again gull a single honest man in Ireland. Lord Lansdowne has been used as a kind of whipping-boy for the Liberal Party, but

Lord Lansdowne's speech* has only brought to the test the system of deceit which has been practised upon the Irish people for the past two years.

---

* Insisting that under the Headings of Agreement, the separation of the Six Counties was to be permanent, unless repealed by a new Act of the Imperial Parliament.

Our deluded people have been shamelessly assured that the last difficulty about Home Rule was gone, and that as soon as the war was over, the Home Rule Act would come into operation automatically for the whole of Ireland, although the men who made that shameful statement had been listening to the Prime Minister (Mr. Asquith) solemnly pledging himself in this House that the Act could never come into operation at all without an Amending Act, and that in any case the notion of ever coercing Ulster into obedience to that Act was unthinkable.

Before Lord Lansdowne made his speech at all, as the Minister for War (Mr. Lloyd George) **has recalled, the Prime Minister announced in this House that the six counties would be definitely struck out of the Home Rule Act, and could never be replaced except by a new Act of this Imperial Parliament, and as the Minister for War reminded us, that announcement was received without a single word of protest by the member for Waterford and his friends, who are so indignantly noisy to-night.**

Sir, if that is not permanence I should like to know what is. Nevertheless, we have the same old word-splitting to-night about the whole agreement being temporary, because no precise guarantee in words was given that Ulster was to be perpetually excluded. No, Sir, but was there any guarantee to Ireland to the contrary? That is the marrow of the whole question—that under the Agreement accepted by the member for Waterford, Ulster was to remain the absolute mistress of her own destinies for the future. Sir E. Carson is the winner, and could afford to be in an amiable humour to-night. In the eloquent speech with which the House is still ringing, he, I have no doubt, quite sincerely proposed an historic shake hands with the member for Waterford on the floor of this House.

Yes, but, sir, that would be a shake hands over the Partition of Ireland, and over the corpse of Ireland as a Nation.

Sir E. Carson can very well afford smooth words, for he is not depending for his own guarantees upon soft words or upon scraps of paper. He has the far more solid guarantee that three-fourths of the representatives of Ireland were ready solemnly to acknowledge that Ulster is a separate State, with separate rights and interests and a separate history— they were quite ready to split our ancient nation into two antagonistic States, which were specially delimited with a view to accumulating in each of them the maximum of racial and religious passions. More than that, he has the guarantee of both the great English Parties that Ulster will never be coerced by England into surrendering that privileged position and going back under the rule of the Board of Erin.

Nothing of the kind could ever be attempted without a special Act of this House for the Coercion of Ulster— an Act which is about as likely as an Act of this House to coerce the people of London to annex themselves to Germany, and this is what is to be the purely temporary and provisional arrangement.

I noticed that the member for Waterford made no allusion to a matter that has been much dangled before us in Ireland. I mean the miracle we were taught to expect from an Imperial Conference hereafter. But the Minister for War did refer to it, and I must say a few words on that subject.

I think I was myself the first who suggested the overseas Ministers as mediators, but how were they to be mediators, if you had decided beforehand the point which is the very kernel of the whole dispute?

The Imperial Conference would be confronted with the fact that by an Act of this House, with the assent of five-sixths of the representatives of Ireland, Ireland had been split up into two different Stales, of different racial origin and of antagonistic creeds, and that that divorce had been pronounced upon the special ground that it was the only way of avoiding civil war. Do you

really want us to believe that those overseas gentlemen confronted with these facts would proceed to order this House to pass
an Act annulling the divorce and would order out an Army to
reconquer Ulster for the Board of Erin? The thing is too farcical.
All this talk of temporary and provisional is the most abominable deceit in a transaction which is one continuous chain of
deceits and treason to the cause of Ireland.

**If Ireland were once dismembered, by the votes of her own
representatives, asthey had fully agreed to dismem-
ber her, that crime could never be undone except by a
bloody revolution.**

I want to say a few words on the second point on which these
negotiations have been broken off. The member for Waterford, I
was glad to see, made no pretence whatever to have the authority of the people of Ireland for these Headings of Agreement.
Sir, this English House of Commons is not the proper venue to
attack the conduct of individual Irish members.

**The proper way and the Constitutional way would be to send
them back to their own constituents for their verdict.**

Their mandate from the country is already more than twelve
months exhausted. Send them back to the country, and at least
give the Irish people some voice in the most tremendous change
that ever was proposed in their destiny, upon the issue which is
practically whether Ireland is to take her life as a Nation with her
own hand. But, Sir, that is not what you democratic and radical
gentlemen were proposing to do according to this agreement.

**On the contrary, you proposed to remove them from all
responsibility to their constituents for several years to
come, and I have not the shadow of a doubt that the
overwhelming reason why this bargain was broken was
that you have been forced to abandon that particular
plan.**

For what was that plan? What you proposed was a coup d'etat, at which Pitt and Castlereagh themselves would have staggered. For Castlereagh only transferred men from one Parliament to another, while you proposed to constitute the same men a Parliament in Dublin and at the same time to let them remain the masters of this House.

You proposed to constitute an Irish Parliament by the simple expedient of transferring 60 of the members of the Party who sit behind me from their Party meeting upstairs in Committee Room 16 to some unburnt house in Dublin.

Instead of sending them back to their constituents, you proposed to set them up as an irresponsible sovereign oligarchy for a minimum of two years and a half without election by anybody, to the indignation and abhorrence of nine-tenths of the Irish race. And it is this caricature of a Parliament, nominated by this House, paid £400 a year apiece out of the English Treasury, even if they should be self-denying enough to refuse themselves any additional remuneration for their services in Dublin—this is the beautiful democratic experiment which would be begotten by Martial Law and would have to be maintained by Martial Law—this is what you are pleased to call making Ireland a Nation once again! This is your way of fighting the battle of the small nationalities—Ireland being one small nationality, which you conspired to make smaller by despoiling her of a province larger and richer than Alsace, and the people, whose liberties and one-fourth of whose soil you were selling away were not to have a voice in the transaction, even the million and a quarter of people who were to be expelled from Ireland were not to have the right of bringing their own representatives to account.

Sir, that hideous plot has failed, but I repeat, the Irish people will never forget nor forgive it to those who were perfectly willing to have carried that plot into effect behind their backs.

The Minister for War (Mr. Lloyd George) is aware that I was not without alternative proposals. These proposals would have infinitely better answered his immediate object by appealing to the imagination of Ireland and America. These proposals would, I believe, have gone nearer to the heart of the member for Trinity College than the Partition of his country, and they would have established the indestructible unity of Ireland as a Nation within a Federation arrangement which would have preserved to Ulster the rights of Imperial citizenship.

It is too late now to go back upon what might have been, or perhaps as the member for Trinity College hinted, it may only be too soon. But I acknowledge, that it has pleased all parties of politicians, English and Irish, in this House and in Ireland, it has pleased them in their wisdom to deprive myself and those with whom I have had the honour of acting, of the slightest power of doing anything effectual under existing conditions to remedy the situation. The work will have to be left to other men in other times, as better men have had to leave it before us. Sir, the real cause of the recent Rebellion was not pro-Germanism, not German gold. The real cause was that you have driven all that is most generous and unselfish among the young men of Ireland into despair of the Constitutional Movement.

And you have done it first by your own bungling or ignorance, or double dealing in this House in your treatment of Home Rule, but above all by the methods by which you have governed Ireland for the past six years in obedience to a secret society of place-hunters, confined to members of one particular creed—a secret society whose sectarian exclusiveness is the negation of the first principle of Irish Nationality. You have filled millions of honest Irish hearts with loathing of Parliamentarianism, English and Irish.

By an inevitable reaction you have raised up a more formi-

dable counter secret society who are at all events pure in their ideals, and who have proved the courage with which they can fight and die like men for these ideals.

If this crippled Parliament of cripples could ever have succeeded in anything, they could only have succeeded in re-establishing the fallen power of this evil Secret Organization of place-jobbers, which has been your undoing as well as Ireland's. But in that you never could or can succeed. It would be too monstrous and unnatural.

You would have against you all those Irish Nationalists who think, all those who are the teachers of the rising generation, and all those who are ready for any sacrifice of liberty or of life for the sake of the old ideals of Irish Nationality, such as we have known it all our lives. Happily for yourselves, the plot has failed, for you would find that you cannot save the Board of Erin, but that you could and would lose, perhaps for ever, any key to the soul of Nationalist Ireland. The day on which this Partition was forced into law, you would be pronouncing the death sentence of the Constitutional Movement, you would be handing over the future public life of Ireland to the Irish Republicans, and you would be once more making the quarrel between Ireland and England an incurable and an everlasting one. Fortunately for yourselves as well as for Ireland, this particular plot at all events for the dismemberment of Ireland is dead and damned to-night, and millions of our race will to-morrow rejoice with all their hearts over its fate.

IV

THE FRAUDULENT "IRISH CONVENTION"

[Speech delivered on May 21st, 1917, in the debate on the proposal of the Prime Minister (Mr. Lloyd George) to summon an Irish Convention.]

MR. WILLIAM O'BRIEN—

The Prime Minister's proposals are contained in two apparently water-tight compartments: The first is the Bill which the Government offered to introduce based on the severance of six Irish counties from the body of Ireland, and that offer could only be met by an immediate and unchangeable negative on the part of the Irish people. You may abuse Longford as much as you like, but Longford has shot the fox—Longford has killed Partition* so far as the Nationalists of Ireland are concerned. The alternative plan which now, after the Prime Minister's speech, remains the only one—the plan of referring to Irishmen themselves the drafting of a Constitution for Ireland—is one which, if it had been adopted six or seven years ago by the Government, must to a certainty have led to a happy settlement so far as anything human is certain. That offer is one which, even now at the half-past eleventh hour, ought not to be dismissed by any man in this House, and especially by any Irishman, without grave and anxious deliberation.

Unfortunately the speech we have just heard from the Hon. Baronet (Sir John Lonsdale), the leader of the Ulster Unionist

---

* At the South Longford Election the Board of Erin candidate had just been defeated by Sinn Féin.

Party, makes it only too plain that the Partition proposals of the Government, as to which neither of the previous speakers (the Prime Minister and Mr. Redmond) has said a single word, remain far the most formidable danger of the situation in Ulster. That being so, Mr. Speaker, unless we are again to yield to the easy optimism and child-like trustfulness which have been the ruin of the Home Rule cause, that fact has got to be grappled with, and if you are ever to understand the real forces you are dealing with in Ireland—as to which you are deplorably—I must in frankness say deplorably— ignorant, you must not really expect us to forget the elaborate system of Partition which the Government, or rather their predecessors, attempted last year to force upon the Irish people. Our British rulers actually imagined they were soothing the national pride of one of the most sensitive races upon earth, while they were all the time wounding to the quick the feelings of every Irish Nationalist, and indeed of every other Irishman as well, with a degree of stupidity that was scarcely exceeded by the worst wrongs of the old times. Because in those old days at all events England acted with her eyes open and with the deliberate purpose to insult and oppress.

You persisted in that scheme of Partition notwithstanding the most earnest remonstrances which some of us could address to you. When the late Prime Minister went to Ireland after the Dublin rising— it was a pity he waited for the Dublin rising to go— the position of our own friends, at all events, was made absolutely clear to him, and it was this: Any amount of concession that would unite Ireland, but Partition, permanent or, as you call it, temporary, never! You persisted with your Partition scheme and you failed. The Government and those Irish representatives who thought fit to act with them were driven from the field by a storm of public fury and horror more universal, I think, than anything I ever witnessed in Ireland; you had scarcely a man in the whole country with you north or south except the place-hunters, and the place-hunters very quickly took to their heels. That lively experience occurred only nine or ten months ago. Yet, here we have, or rather up to to-night had, the Prime Minister coming up again to offer us a Bill which in a slightly more gilded form is the self-same nostrum of Partition which was rejected last summer as a burning insult by almost every honest man of the Irish race.

The only difference between the two schemes which is worth a moment's discussion is the pretext that some shadow of national unity is preserved to Ireland by this so-called Council of Ireland. That device does some credit to the Prime Minister's ingenuity, but, Sir, it is of no more real value as a preservative of the integrity of Ireland than if you were to put in a proviso that the Hon Baronet and his Ulster men might still travel up to Dublin to attend the Punchestown races. The work assigned to this Council is too trivial for words. Indeed it could absolutely do no work at all without the leave of the Hon. Baronet and his Ulster Party in this House, who would command a majority of fifteen to six Nationalists in the Ulster delegation. The proposal is luckily too insignificant to be really irritating. Otherwise the only effect could be to add an additional complication by setting up a new and irresponsible dual control in Dublin to review and criticize every act of the unfortunate mutilated Dublin Parliament. I cannot suppose the Prime Minister really desired to add insult to the injury of the exclusion of the six counties by establishing the Ulster Party in this House in addition as a rival authority to snub the unfortunate Dublin Parliament at every turn. But the truth is, the whole thing is so ridiculously unworkable that the only practical purpose of any kind it could serve would be to throw dust in the eyes of the American people and to keep President Wilson in good humour.

Sir, the essence of the Government's first proposal is Partition in a more insidious form. Its essence is a renewal of the intolerable insult that Ireland is not one nation but two. Whether our country is to be mutilated county by county, or by what, in the language of the butchers, is called the clean cut, the result would be to split Ireland asunder as surely as if what the Prime Minister proposed to us was to fight another battle of the Boyne.

Sir, we had no difficulty in telling you four years ago, as we are telling you now, that the Irish Nation will never submit to any such scheme as long as grass grows and water runs. What would be your own feelings if the Germans proposed to you as a condition of peace that you should cede to them—I won't say six of the richest counties on your southern coast, but that you should cede to them even temporarily as you say—even for five years—the smallest parcel of the sacred soil of England—say Westminster Abbey. Mr. Speaker, Westminster Abbey does not contain an ounce of dust more sacred for you than do for us the shrines and graves and battlefields which we are asked to surrender to an Orange Free State as a visible symbol that the integrity of Ireland as a nation has ceased to exist. No, sir— better, as Cardinal Logue said, better let us wait for fifty years longer, and I tell you you will have to wait for fifty centuries longer before you will ever get the Irish nation to cut up the land of their fathers either by the clean cut or county by county, under some preposterous system of a majority of two or three hundred jerrymandered or corrupted votes.

I do not at all say that if the Irish people were to treat you as unscrupulously as they have been treated themselves, they would not close with the offer of the Government, such as it is, but they could only do so with the determination to work it in a spirit of sleepless hostility to England and to those Irishmen who might attempt to organize that abominable caricature of an Irish Parliament. Sir, the Irish people are not sufficiently good hypocrites to play a Machiavellian game of that kind, and it is just because we desire peace, and genuine peace, between the two countries that

I tell you straight that for the few hundred placemen you might content, you would be making enemies of millions of the best men and women of the Irish race.

I know all your difficulties. Unhappily after the speech we have listened to from the Hon. Baronet they may seem at this stage all but insurmountable. But these difficulties are mainly due to your own feebleness and double-dealing—to the feebleness and double-dealing of the late Home Rule Government and their Irish allies. They could never make up their minds either to conciliate Ulster while there was yet time to do it, nor to enforce their own law under the Parliament Act. We shall hear plenty of complaints now of the speech of the Hon. Baronet, the leader of the Ulster Party, but where is the use of complaining if he and his Ulster men take their stand on the six counties, and take advantage of their knowledge that they never will be compelled to obey the law like other people? Yes, but whose fault is that? The Home Rule Government and, unfortunately, their Irish auxiliaries first offered them four counties, and then advanced their bid to six. They passed a so-called Home Rule Act with the public stipulation that it was never to be put in force without an Amending Act, which would repeal it in its most vital particular. They passed it further subject to the solemn assurance of the Home Rule Prime Minister that the notion of Ulster being ever compelled to obey that Statute was unthinkable—Sir, to my mind, a monstrously unconstitutional doctrine. It would be the death of the first principle of all democratic government. But that was then common ground all round in every Party in this House except in our own small camp, and the foulest insults were hurled at us in this House for daring to make even the most modest protest. Sir. how can you be surprised if the Ulster men have now taken you at your own solemn word? You never proffered a single concession to the Ulstermen while they were still unarmed, and while even in this House they were still amenable enough to reason and to conciliation. Neither did you attempt to dispute their right to arm in order to bid defiance to your Parliament Act with arms in their hands. If we clear our minds of cant we all know that nothing happened in Dublin in the rising of Easter week that would not have happened in Belfast on a much larger scale if you had attempted to enforce the law there. It is all your own doing, and, unfortunately, the doing of five-sixths of Ireland's own representatives as well, and it is this miserable collapse of Parliamentarianism which is responsible for the Dublin rising—which is responsible for the Roscommon election and the Longford election, and which is responsible for the contempt and hatred of Parliamentary methods which has unquestionably taken possession of far the largest portion of the uncorrupted youth of Ireland.

Sir, I turn with relief to the Prime Minister's alternative plan which is now the only hope. No man in this House could like to think that the last word has been spoken in this great matter of the reconciliation of the two countries which has been brought so marvellously far towards success. For my own part, a Home Rule Settlement, by the consent of all sections and persuasions of our countrymen, has been the one—I can truly say the one and only object of my political life for the past fifteen years. It is the only hope which could induce me to linger for twenty-four hours more in Irish public life, such as it has become. It would be affectation to deny that this alternative plan of the Government might well make the ears of some of us tingle with satisfaction because the Government have at long last begun to find out that the only real way out of the Irish difficulty lies through those principles of Conference. Conciliation and Consent which we have spent the last five years in preaching to deaf ears in this House. Our unforgivable sin was that we only counted seven against seventy in the Division Lobbies. But let that pass. Undoubtedly the declaration now made by the Govern-

ment that to Irishmen themselves should be left the settlement
of their country's legislative and fiscal future is one of the most
momentous announcements that ever was made in this House.
It is the resumption and the completion of Mr. Wyndham's historic declaration in the same sense in 1902, which put an end
to the agrarian war. There are only one or two observations by
which I should like to qualify my wholehearted approval of the
general principle. The first is only as to a matter of practical procedure, but it will be found to be one of vital importance if
the Government really mean business—if, as I trust, this is an
honest effort and is not mere playing to the American gallery
for war purposes. The Prime Minister unfortunately has made it
plain that by the term Convention he means the assembling of a
large body of men. Well, Sir, that will involve you at once in almost insuperable difficulties as to the selection or election of the
members. However you manage it the cry is quite sure to arise
from one side or the other that it is a packed Convention, a term
of not very fragrant memory in Ireland. For instance, the hon.
Member for Waterford has just thrown out the suggestion that
you should call in the County Councils, Corporations, District
Councils and so on. Well, sir, if there is one fact notorious in
Ireland it is that these bodies were elected five years ago and have
long exhausted their mandate, and do not in the least degree
represent the present state of public opinion in Ireland.

The selection of this Convention would in point of fact give
you as much trouble as a general election, without satisfying anybody. Then even if you had this big Convention assembled, you
would have no end of hot-headed partisans rushing in with their
own particular plans and fads, and you would find it impossible
within any reasonable time to reach what you require, which is
a prompt, succinct, consistent and practicable agreement. This
morning's *Times* wisely warned you that the analogy from the
case of the more phlegmatic people of South Africa on which

the Prime Minister dwelt is a wholly illusory one— not much wiser than the English bull which has suggested General Smuts as the principal personage in a purely Irish assembly. From my experience of Irish affairs, which is at all events one of considerable length, you will I believe find that the only possibility of a prompt agreement is among a small number of men, and that its success must depend not upon the personality of the men, but upon their agreement being of such a character as to commend itself to the overwhelming sense of the community. The other observation I should like to make is that I hope we may take it for granted from the Prime Minister's speech to-night that the mandate of this Convention, or whatever you may call, will be entirely separate from the views of Partition that were to be embodied in the proposed Government Bill—in other words, that the alternative plan must be read independently of the views enunciated in the first part of the Prime Minister's letter. Otherwise, any Convention, such as you contemplate, if it ever assembles at all, will either break up on the question of Partition, or if it be packed with place-hunters will end in some Partition compromise, which will be repudiated with fury by the country.

Up to the last moment my friends and myself urged in the competent quarters as we have done for the past five years that it is not in this House but in Ireland the foundations of any real settlement must be laid. But we warned them that all our suggestions were based upon the principle that although a conference would of course, in courtesy, listen to any discussion, be the cost what it may, for your sakes as well as for our own, Partition in any shape is inadmissible and impossible. What we suggested was that the Government should begin by inviting a small Conference of Irishmen in Ireland, not necessarily composed of the leaders of any existing party or section. In this I am glad to be in entire agreement with the hon. member for Waterford, although he probably would not go so far as myself when I say the less the Conference would have of party leaders the better, because I am afraid it is not the Irish people but the leaders of all existing parties and sections who are mainly responsible for the whole mischief. I do not, of course, make any exception whatever. I admit that the present situation in Ireland is one of mere chaos, and that nobody—literally no politician—is at the present moment in a position to answer for the action of the Irish people.

But it would be still not at all difficult to hit upon the names of a dozen eminent Irishmen—men of broadmindedness and imagination and toleration wide enough to embrace all political sects of our countrymen from the most moderate to the most extreme.*

If you could assemble a dozen such men around a friendly council table, they could be depended upon not to separate in such a crisis for our country without some great and memorable

---

* A good deal that went on behind the scenes at the time cannot yet be made public, but there is no reason why one panel of typical names for the Conference which I submitted to the Cabinet on May 24th, 1919, at their request, may not now be disclosed, viz., the Lord Mayor of Dublin (Alderman O'Neill), the Protestant Primate, the Catholic Archbishop of Dublin, the Marquess of Londonderry, the Marquess of Ormonde, General Sir Hubert Gough, Major "Willie" Redmond. M.P.; the Earl of Shaftesbury, the Earl of Dunraven, Viscount Northcliffe, Mr. William Martin Murphy, Mr. Hugh Barrie, M.P., and two representatives of Sinn Féin. Some of these names would have sounded startlingly at the time. But by the light of events that have occurred since few reasonable men will now doubt that if a Conference thus composed had then met, they would not have separated without an agreement. Still fewer will doubt that if their agreement had been submitted to a Referendum or Plebiscite of the Irish people, in the circumstances then existing, it would have been endorsed by a majority so overpowering as to make any further resistance in any quarter unthinkable. I was in a position at the time to guarantee that, at a Conference of this character, Sinn Féin would not be unrepresented.

national agreement upon some such non-partitionist and Federationist lines as I have again and again indicated in this House and outside it. Let me add that the chances of an agreement would be all the better among all classes of Irishmen north and south the further the Conference would travel away from the existing Act upon the Statute-book, which has really become a bitter laughing-stock throughout the country.

Well, suppose you had an Irish agreement. We suggested as the second stage that it should be submitted to the Imperial Cabinet, including the Premiers of the Over Seas Dominions. For that tribunal there might now be substituted the hybrid committee of an Imperial character which the Prime Minister contemplated in case his Bill received a second reading under the presidency of some man of the type of Mr. Speaker, if indeed a second such man is to be found. Once you had secured an Irish agreement thus splendidly fortified, the democratic thing would be to submit it frankly by Referendum to the whole Irish people, and then by all means place on the Irish people the responsibility for its acceptance or rejection, for under a Referendum the masses of the Irish people would have a voice such as they can never have under your nominated or selected Convention. If, as I am very sure, the response to a Referendum should be an all but universal chorus of acceptance and relief from every substantial element in the country, including the bulk of the great Protestant and Dissenting communities—well, then, let the Government do what the Home Rule Government ought to have done five or six years ago, let them adopt the agreement as their own, and let them publicly announce that they will if necessary go to the country and appeal for the sovereign authority of the electorate if any small section of merely irrational irreconcilables at either extreme should still attempt to block the way. I am speaking of a small and irrational minority. I do not, of course, speak of the Unionist body in bulk, and of course if you were to attempt

Partition in any shape you would be dealing not with an irrational minority but with practically the entire Irish race, fifteen or twenty millions of them, and you would find yourself up against that rock of Irish nationality against which all the force of England has spent itself in vain for the past eight hundred years.

What I want the House to mark is that you have never yet tried any of the things I mention. You have never called the Irish people into consultation. You have never called the electorate into consultation. You have never offered any concession to Ulster except one which would call upon us with our own hand to take the very life of our motherland as a nation. You have abdicated the first function of democratic government in favour of the right of rebellion, whether in Belfast or in Dublin, and if the Prime Minister's first proposal could pass you would be simply extending the area of the next insurrection to Derry and Tyrone and Enniskillen.

I don't deny—Mark Tapley himself could scarcely deny—that at this time of day you may fail to produce any general Irish agreement even through such a Conference as we propose. You have let one golden opportunity after another slip through your fingers. It is tragic to think that if the Government had only made their alternative proposal six or seven years ago, and if the Irish bishops, Catholic and Protestant, had only then issued their recent manifesto, all these troubles might have been long ago blessedly composed, and the whole course of the war might have been very considerably altered. It may quite possibly be now too late. But the point is, you have never yet tried it. That is the astounding fact, but fact it is. The Prime Minister's own letter confesses it, and fail how you might, you could never at the worst reach a more humiliating position than you occupy to-day before the nations of the world, confessing that you have incurred obligations to Ireland which you are in honour bound to discharge and that you cannot do it.

I am still not altogether without hope that a Government which had the grit to tackle all the might of Germany unflinchingly may no longer stand shivering before two opposite sets of extremists in the Irish seas. Unfortunately the Prime Minister's speech which, I am afraid, lacked a good deal of his usual magnetic attraction, did not afford very much evidence of the fearlessness and high purpose which alone can pluck a successful Irish settlement out of the dangers in which the miserable bungling of the politicians has entangled us. If you break down now—I pray you not to delude yourself on this point—if you break down now, you will not kill the Irish cause, but you will kill any reasonable chance for our time of reconstructing the Constitutional Movement upon an honest basis. You will kill all Irish belief in this House or in any Party in it. You will set up the right of Rebellion, whether for the Covenanters or the Sinn Féiners, as the only arbiter left in Irish affairs. You will justly make Parliamentary methods even more despised and detested than they are at the present moment by the young men of Ireland. You will force the Irish people, sorely against their will, to turn their eyes altogether away from this Parliament to the International Peace Congress. I daresay it will turn out to be an equally hopeless mirage, but at all events, you will have left the Irish people no alternative except to haunt your path at that Congress and to join all the other small nations of Europe in a final appeal for freedom to that supreme tribunal of European and American democracy and humanity.

APPENDIX

CORRESPONDENCE WITH THE PRIME MINISTER

10 DOWNING STREET,
WHITEHALL, S.W.,

13th June, 1917.

DEAR MR. O'BRIEN—Pursuant to my statement in the House of Commons on the 11th instant, I now have the satisfaction of requesting you to nominate two representatives of the Party under your leadership who may be invited to serve as members of the Convention.

With the terms of reference you are familiar. I stated them in my letter to you of the 16th May in these words:—

"Would it be too much to hope that Irishmen of all creeds and parties might meet together in a Convention for the purpose of drafting a Constitution for their country which should secure a just balance of all the opposing interests, and finally compose the unhappy discords which have so long distracted Ireland and impeded its harmonious development."

I further referred to them in the House of Commons as follows:—

"The Government, therefore, propose to summon immediately, on behalf of the Crown, a Convention of representative Irishmen in Ireland, to submit to the British Government a Constitution for the future government of Ireland within the Empire."

I shall be glad to learn as soon as may be convenient to you the names of the gentlemen to whom invitations should now be sent.

Yours very truly,
D. LLOYD GEORGE.

WILLIAM O'BRIEN, ESQ., M.P.,
House of Commons, S.W.

MALLOW,
June 18*th,* 1917.

DEAR MR. LLOYD GEORGE—To my deep disappointment, the details of how "The Irish Convention" is to be composed confirm the apprehensions which I endeavoured to express in the House of Commons. The rejoicing excited by the courageous Amnesty for the Insurrection of last year cannot be allowed to blind the country to the danger.

1. While the Government have nominally adopted the principle of allowing the future Constitution of Ireland to be settled by agreement among Irishmen themselves, they have done so under conditions which render that principle a nullity. There can be little or no hope that a Convention constituted as the Government have directed can arrive at any decision except some hateful bargain for the partition of the country under a plausible disguise. To attribute the blame for such a decision or for the failure to arrive at any better one to the Irish people would be little short of an outrage upon Ireland, and would be a gross imposition on the credulity of friendly nations abroad.

2. The proposed Convention would both be too large to make a prompt and carefully-considered agreement practicable, and too small for a National Assembly purporting to represent all the great interests concerned. The fact that the scheme excludes from any direct representation whatever the 400,000 Ulster Nationalists whom any Partition proposal hitherto contemplated would cut off from their country; the agricultural and urban labourers, comprising one-third of the Irish population; the great farming interest in the area of the Rural District Councils, and the Universities and other teaching professions—must surely make it unnecessary to emphasise the latter point.

3. While the politicians' organizations are in appearance restricted to a delegation of five apiece, the pretence is, to the

knowledge of everybody in Ireland, a misleading one. The twin organizations of the Irish Parliamentary Party—the most powerful of the two being of a secret and rigidly sectarian character— would command a majority of the Convention as disciplined as if directly delegated by these organizations, and, in the event of "a deal" with the Ulster Unionist body of at least twenty-five delegates, would represent an overwhelming vote for some scheme of Partition, such as the two Nationalist organizations referred to strove hard last year to force upon the Nationalists of Ireland, and have never since categorically pledged themselves to renounce. Their leaders have, on the contrary, on more than one recent occasion expressed their regret that the Partition bargain of last year did not succeed.

I do not impugn the sincerity of those who may believe any compromise would be better than failure to secure an agreement, but am absolutely convinced, for my own part, that Partition under any disguise would mean the destruction of the ideal of Ireland a Nation, and could not, indeed, be enforced at all without bloodshed and disorder.

4. The solid majority—apart even from the aid of the direct nominees of the Government—which the Irish Parliamentary Party would thus be able to cast in favour of any such Partitionist compromise— would consist principally of Mayors and Chairmen of County Councils, all of whom were the choice of the Board of Erin wing of the Ancient Order of Hibernians and of the United Irish League, and could not have been elected without the imprimatur of these organisations. This fact might not be material if the Board of Erin Hibernians and the United Irish League could still pretend to enjoy the confidence of the country; but their leaders have owned that the contrary is the truth, and, as a matter of fact, have not attempted to hold a free public meeting anywhere throughout the country for more than a year past. The local governing bodies, like the Irish Parliamentary Par-

ty themselves, have outstayed their mandate from the country by several years. The greater number of those whom the Government arrangements will constitute a majority of the Convention would quite certainly be defeated if they were obliged to face their constituents at the polls.* The will of the people is, therefore, rendered powerless to control the secret deliberations of the Convention, and would be forced to find other and regrettable means of resisting any such Partitionist compromise, as there is only too substantial reason to apprehend.

5. On the other hand, while my friends and myself would welcome the most generous representation of the unofficial Unionist population of Ireland, the Government scheme ensures to the official Ulster Unionist Council a full third of the voting power of the Convention—under the direction, moreover, of a Committee not present at the Convention, but specially nominated by the Council to supervise its proceedings from outside. The terms of the Resolution under which the Ulster Unionist Council consented to enter the Convention make it clear that they have only done so as a War measure, and, relying upon the assurances of the Government that they need fear no Parliamentary pressure if they should adhere to their demand for the exclusion of the six counties as a minimum—a demand, indeed, which was conceded to them last year by the Irish Parliamentary Party. It is consequently obvious that the chances of any agreement by the Ulster Unionist Council other than one based on the separation of the six counties are all but hopelessly handicapped from the start, and the temptation dangerously increased to those Nationalist politicians who have already committed themselves to dismemberment.

---

* As a matter of fact, only one of the seventy-five Hibernians who constituted the majority of "the Irish Convention" survived the verdict of the people at the polls.

6. As you are aware, my friends and myself have long since urged upon the Cabinet a constructive proposal, by which alone, in our judgment, any agreement involving a genuine settlement of the Irish difficulty can now be obtained, viz., a small Conference of responsible Irishmen, on the Land Conference model, to draft the headings of a project of Self-government for Ireland such as would guarantee a future of the fullest security and power to the Unionists of Ulster and of the South as well in the government of our common native land; such agreement, if arrived at, to be submitted to a vote of the people of Ireland by way of Referendum.

Recent experience has convinced me more deeply than ever that it is to a small Round Table Conference of thoughtful and competent Irishmen, and not to a heterogeneous assembly, mostly composed of pre-committed partisan politicians, we must look for the materials on which the country might with confidence be called upon for a judgment, and that a Referendum, giving the whole mass of the population a direct and influential voice, would be the only means of eliciting a decision so overpowering as to put an end to all further controversy among rational men.

It is because I am driven to the conclusion that the Government scheme, while making a specious appearance of adopting the Conference method, in reality adopts it only to destroy its efficacy—because it forbids all reasonable hope of any agreement other than one which could only inflame and intensify Irish discontent, and because it would most unjustly cast upon the Irish people the blame for a failure of the Government's own producing—that I have made up my mind, with reluctance, and, indeed, with poignant personal sorrow, that I must decline to undertake any responsibility in connection with a Convention so constituted.

Yours very truly,

WILLIAM O'BRIEN.

RIGHT HON. D. LLOYD GEORGE, M.P., *Prime Minister.*